THE PROFESSOR

THE MERMAID

Published by
Westland Books, a division of Nasadiya Technologies Private Limited, in 2025
No. 269/2B, First Floor, 'Irai Arul', Vimalraj Street, Nethaji Nagar, Alapakkam Main Road, Maduravoyal, Chennai 600095

in co-publishing arrangement with
Shakti Comics, The Search House, B-23/C1, Sector 62, Noida, UP

Westland and the Westland logo are the trademarks of Nasadiya Technologies Private Limited, or its affiliates.

ISBN: 978-93-7197-076-1

10 9 8 7 6 5 4 3 2

Created by E.C. Segar

Written & Illustrated by Bud Sagendorf

Cover Art & Colours: Avishek Biswas

Editor: Vikramaditya

SHAKTI COMICS

DID I HEAR PROFESSOR O.G. WATASNOZZLE ?
YEAH!
©2000 by King Features Syndicate, Inc. World rights reserved.
I WAS BEGINNIN' TO WON'ER IF HE WAS STILL IN THERE!
BUD SAGENDORF
?
I KNEW HE WAS... HE'S BEEN CLEANING HIS PLATE EVERY DAY!!
KEEP OUT!
FEED HERE
3-28

WHAT DO YOU THINK THE PERFESSOR HAS BEEN DOING ?
THINKING!
©2000 by King Features Syndicate, Inc. World rights reserved.
HOW DOES YA KNOW ?
3-29
BY THE FIRST LIGHT... IT'S BEEN ON NIGHT AND DAY FOR THREE MONTHS!
THINKING
HUNGRY
SLEEPING
!
?
- PRIVATE -
O.G. WATASNOZZLE
KEEP OUT
BUD SAGENDORF

WHAT'S ALL THE EXCITEMENT ?
THE PERFESSOR IS MAKIN' NOISE!
©2000 by King Features Syndicate, Inc. World rights reserved.
CLICK!
HE'S COMIN' OUT!
MY ATOMIC BRAIN HAS FOUND THE SOLUTION TO ALL OF THE WORLD'S PROBLEMS!!
I AM INDEED A GENIUS!
BUD SAGENDORF
3-30

IF YOU KNOW HOW TO LICK THE WORLD'S PROBLEMS YOU'LL BE FAMOUS!
DON'T BE SILLY!
©2000 by King Features Syndicate, Inc. World rights reserved.
BETTER THAN THAT!
?
WE WILL BOTH BE FAMOUS!!
WE?
3-31
BUD SAGENDORF

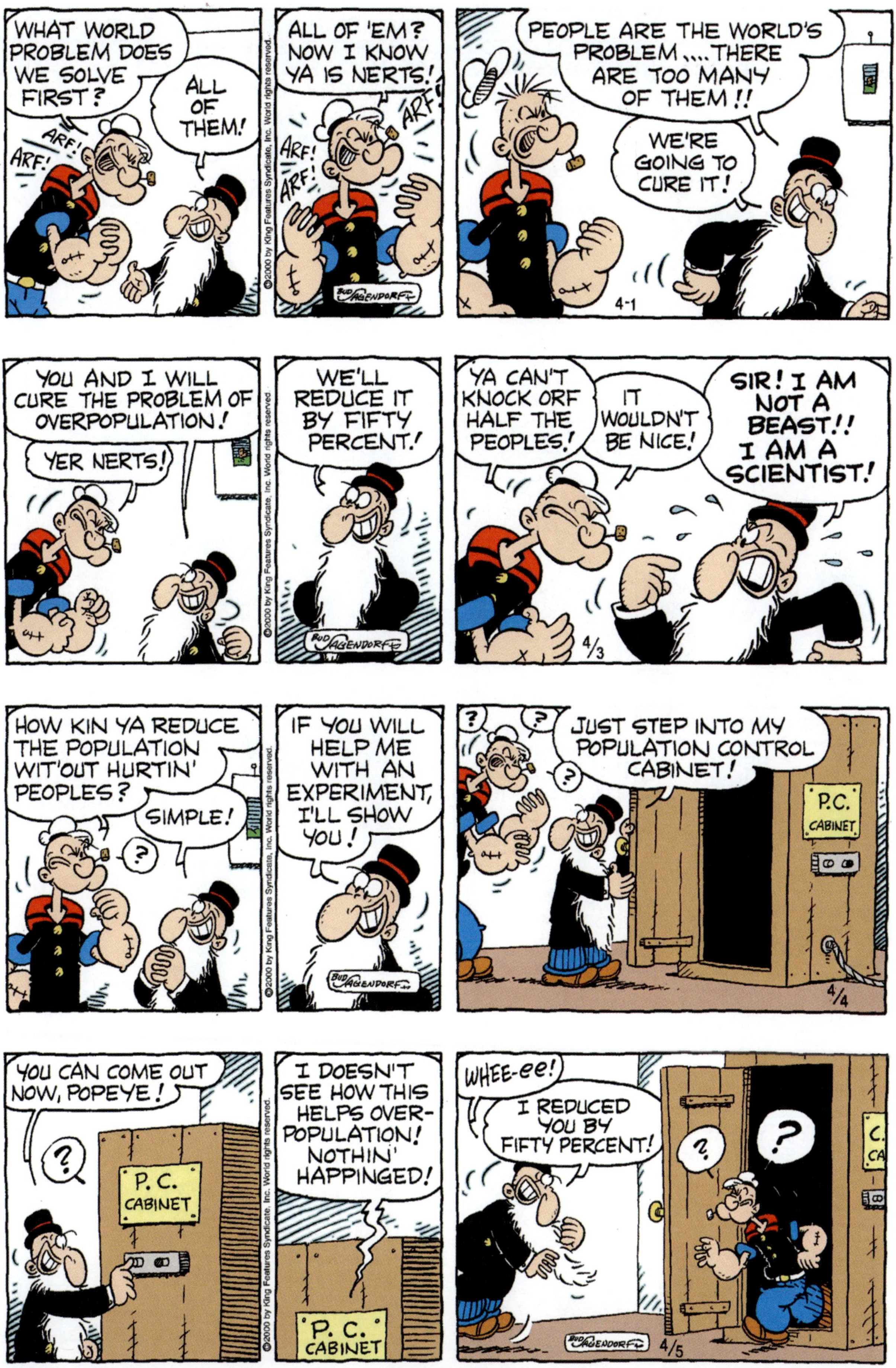
WHAT WORLD PROBLEM DOES WE SOLVE FIRST?
ARF! ARF!
ALL OF THEM!
©2000 by King Features Syndicate, Inc. World rights reserved.
ALL OF 'EM? NOW I KNOW YA IS NERTS!
ARF! ARF! ARF!
BUD SAGENDORF
PEOPLE ARE THE WORLD'S PROBLEM.... THERE ARE TOO MANY OF THEM!!
WE'RE GOING TO CURE IT!
4-1
YOU AND I WILL CURE THE PROBLEM OF OVERPOPULATION!
YER NERTS!
©2000 by King Features Syndicate, Inc. World rights reserved.
WE'LL REDUCE IT BY FIFTY PERCENT!
BUD SAGENDORF
YA CAN'T KNOCK ORF HALF THE PEOPLES!
IT WOULDN'T BE NICE!
SIR! I AM NOT A BEAST!! I AM A SCIENTIST!
4/3
HOW KIN YA REDUCE THE POPULATION WIT'OUT HURTIN' PEOPLES?
SIMPLE!
?
©2000 by King Features Syndicate, Inc. World rights reserved.
IF YOU WILL HELP ME WITH AN EXPERIMENT, I'LL SHOW YOU!
BUD SAGENDORF
? ? ?
JUST STEP INTO MY POPULATION CONTROL CABINET!
P.C. CABINET
4/4
YOU CAN COME OUT NOW, POPEYE!
?
P. C. CABINET
©2000 by King Features Syndicate, Inc. World rights reserved.
I DOESN'T SEE HOW THIS HELPS OVER-POPULATION! NOTHIN' HAPPINGED!
P. C. CABINET
WHEE-ee!
I REDUCED YOU BY FIFTY PERCENT!
? ?
BUD SAGENDORF
4/5

YOU SHRUNK ME!
I DEPOPULATED YOU!
©2000 by King Features Syndicate, Inc. World rights reserved.
I'M GOING TO DO IT TO EVERYONE!
WHEN PEOPLE ARE REDUCED FIFTY PERCENT, THERE WILL BE TWICE AS MUCH FOOD AND LAND FOR EVERY-ONE!
?
4/6
BUD SAGENDORF

YA PROVED YA COULD SHRINK ME... NOW MAKE ME BIG!
IMPOSSIBLE!
©2000 by King Features Syndicate, Inc. World rights reserved.
WHA'CHA MEAN?
?
SIR, I AM A MAN OF SCIENCE! I **DO** THINGS... I DON'T **UNDO** THEM!!
!
4/7
BUD SAGENDORF

IS POPEYE HOME?
HE'S IN THE PROFESSOR'S ROOM!
©2000 by King Features Syndicate, Inc. World rights reserved.
YOO-HOO! POPEYE!
COME IN, OLIVE!
4/8
WHAT HAPPENED TO YOU?
I GOT ME PERSUMAL POPULATION REDUCED BY FIFTY PERCENT!
BUD SAGENDORF

YOU'RE NO BIGGER THAN A CHILD!
THE PERFESSOR SHRUNK ME!
©2000 by King Features Syndicate, Inc. World rights reserved.
YOU'RE DISGUSTING! TELL HIM TO ENLARGE YOU!!
4/10
?
?
GULP!
HE CAN'T! I YAM STUCK THIS WAY!
HIS MACHINE ONLY WORKS ONE WAY!
BUD SAGENDORF

DOES YA STILL WANT TO GO FER A WALK WIT' ME ?
I GUESS SO!
?
©2000 by King Features Syndicate, Inc. World rights reserved.
HM?
?
?
?
4/11
DON'T YOU THINK YOU SHOULD ASK YOUR FATHER IF IT'S ALL RIGHT?
?
!
BUD SAGENDORF

LE'S GO FER OUR WALK!
ER--?
?
©2000 by King Features Syndicate, Inc. World rights reserved.
ON ONE CONDITION!!
?
4/12
BUD SAGENDORF
HE'S A NEIGHBOR'S CHILD!
?

SINCE THE PERFESSOR SHRUNK ME, EVERY-ONE TREATS ME LIKE A CHILD!
©2000 by King Features Syndicate, Inc. World rights reserved.
PHOOEY!!
?
?
AHOY, PAPPY... KIN YOU REACH A CAN OF SPINACH FER ME?
4/13
BUD SAGENDORF

WHA' TH'--?
BERF!
4/14
©2000 by King Features Syndicate, Inc. World rights reserved.
WHA'S WRONG WIT' YER DORG, SWEE'PEA?
BUD SAGENDORF
?
BERF!
BERF!
HE WANTS TO PLAY! HE THINKS YER A LI'L BOY KID!

HERE COMES WIMPY... HE WILL BE SUSPRIZED I HAS BEEN SHRUNK!
©2000 by King Features Syndicate, Inc. World rights reserved.
AHOY, WIMPY!
HELP!
GET ME A DOCTOR! I'VE GROWN INTO A GIANT!
ARF! ARF! ARF! ARF!
4/15
BUD SAGENDORF
IT'S A SHOCK TO SEE YOU THE SIZE OF A CHILD!
THE PERFESSOR DID IT!
©2000 by King Features Syndicate, Inc. World rights reserved
HE SHRUNKED ME!
BUD SAGENDORF
GULP!
I HOPE HE DOESN'T TRY IT ON MY TUMMY!
!
4-17
I CAN'T GO DOWN-TOWN WITH YOU... YOU LOOK LIKE A CHILD!
I YAM YER MAN!
©2000 by King Features Syndicate, Inc. World rights reserved.
I DON'T WANT TO BE LAUGHED AT!
?
DON'T TURN TOO QUICK.... THESE STILTS IS TRICKY!
4-18
BUD SAGENDORF
SNIFF! YA BRINGS BACK MEMORIES, SON!
'AT'S 'CAUSE I GOT SHRUNKED!
©2000 by King Features Syndicate, Inc. World rights reserved.
YA LOOKS LIKE WHEN YA WAS A LI'L BOY!
SNIFF!
I REMEMBERS I DIDN'T SPANK YA FER BLOWIN' BUBBLES WIT' ME PIPE!
BAD BOY!!
?
SPLAT!
SPLAT!
SPLAT!
BUD SAGENDORF
4-19

I WANTS A BOX OF CANDY FER MISS OYL!
CHOC
©2000 by King Features Syndicate, Inc. World rights reserved.
HERE YOU ARE, CUTIE!
-AND HERE'S A LOLLIPOP FOR YOU, SONNY!
FUDGE
CHOC
4-20
BUD SAGENDORF
IT'S NICE OF YOU TO TAKE ME TO THE MOVIES!
YOU IS ME SWEET PATOOTY!
©2000 by King Features Syndicate, Inc. World rights reserved.
I'LL GET THE TICKETS!
?
ONE ADULT AND ONE CHILD!
?
!
4-21
BUD SAGENDORF
I DEMAND YOU MAKE POPEYE TALL AGAIN... I CAN'T STAND HIM BEING A LITTLE SHRIMP!
©2000 by King Features Syndicate, Inc. World rights reserved.
I MADE HIM THE SAME HEIGHT AS MYSELF!
!
THAT'S WHAT I SAID.... HE'S DISGUSTING!!
?
4-22
BUD SAGENDORF
HEY, KID!
I AIN'T NO KID!
4-24
©2000 by King Features Syndicate, Inc. World rights reserved.
OF COURSE YOU'RE NOT... YOU'RE A GREAT BIG MAN!
HA! HA! HA! HA!
?
?
IT MUST BE THE VITAMINS THEY FEED KIDS TODAY!
BUD SAGENDORF

DO YOU REALIZE WHAT DAY THIS IS ?
YEAH... TUESDAY!
©2000 by King Features Syndicate, Inc. World rights reserved.
WHA'S SO IMPORTINK ABOUT TODAY ?
IN A FEW DAYS YOU HAVE TO FIGHT BRUTUS IN THE RING FOR THE ANNUAL SALT-WATER CHAMPIONSHIP!
BLOW ME DOWN! ARF! ARF! I FERGOT!
ARF!
4-25
BUD SAGENDORF

ARF! ARF! I FERGOT ALL ABOUT ME SPRIZE-FIGHT WIT' BRUTUS!
!
ARF!
ARF!
©2000 by King Features Syndicate, Inc. World rights reserved.
IT AIN'T IMPORTINK... I BEATS HIM EVERY YEAR!
BUD SAGENDORF
YOU'RE ALSO FORGETTING THAT YOU ARE NOW THE SIZE OF A SMALL CHILD!
?
?
4-26

IN A FEW DAYS I HAS TA FIGHT BRUTUS FER THE ANNUAL SALT-WATER CHAMPIONSHIP!
YOU ALWAYS WIN!
©2000 by King Features Syndicate, Inc. World rights reserved.
BUT YOU SHRUNKED ME... I AIN'T NO BIGGER THAN A LI'L KID!
?
!
!
?
AH, YES.... THE SACRIFICES OF SCIENCE!
YOU'LL JUST HAVE TO LOSE!
4-27
BUD SAGENDORF

YOU CAN'T FIGHT POPEYE IN THE RING!
WHY NOT?
©2000 by King Features Syndicate, Inc. World rights reserved.
IT WOULDN'T BE FAIR! HE'S SHRUNK! HE'S NO BIGGER THAN A CHILD!
SOB!
?
WHEEE--eee!! WONDERFUL! THIS IS GOING TO BE MY YEAR!!
4-28
BUD SAGENDORF

I NEEDS ROAD-WORK TA BEAT BRUTUS THIS YEAR!
PUFF! PUFF!
OUT OF THE WAY, KID!
THUMP! THUMP! THUMP!
4-29
HA! HA!
LET A MAN PASS!!
BRUTUS
?
PUFF!
YOU CAN'T FIGHT BRUTUS, YOU'RE NO BIGGER THAN A TEN-YEAR-OLD!
I MAY BE MINIATURIZED, BUT I YAM STILL A MAN!
IF YOU INSIST ON BEING STUBBORN I'LL ---
?
--I'LL--I'LL SPANK YOU!!
BLOW ME DOWN!
?
?
5-1
I'D LIKE TO PLACE A WAGER ON YOUR FIGHT WITH BRUTUS!
!
5-2
COULD YOU LOAN ME A FEW THOUSAND?
AFTER YOU LOSE, I WILL COLLECT A FORTUNE!
?
?
WIMPY WANTS TA BET AGAINST ME IN ME FIGHT WIT' BRUTUS!
EVERY-ONE IS!
WHERE IS YOU RUNNIN' TO?
?
!
?
TO THE BANK TO DRAW OUT MY LIFE SAVINGS!
5-3

WHAT'S WRONG WITH YOU, GRAN'SON?
I YAM THINKIN' ABOUT ME FIGHT!
I'VE BEEN THINKING TOO!
?
?
YOU BE SURE YOUR LIFE INSURANCE IS PAID BEFORE IT STARTS!
?
5-4
HAS YOU BEEN FIGHTIN'?
?
YEAH!
5-5
A GANG OF TOUGHS SAID YOU COULDN'T BEAT BRUTUS THIS YEAR
I CORRECTED 'EM!
YOU IS THE ONLY ONE WHAT HAS FAITH IN ME!
WHERE DO YOU THINK YOU'RE GOING?
INTO THE FIGHT!
SCRAM!! KIDS AIN'T ALLOWED!
!
?
ARENA
YER NERTS! I YAM THE MAIN EVENT!
POPEYE
5-6
TONIGHT'S MAIN EVENT IS A FIGHT TO THE FINISH FOR THE SEAMAN'S WATER-FRONT CHAMPIONSHIP!
BETWEEN BRUTUS THE TERRIBLE AND --
YEAH!
-HA! HA! THE MINIATURIZED TEMPORARY TITLEHOLDER-POPEYE THE LITTLE!
?
HA! HA! HA! HA! HA! HA! HA! HA! HA! HA!
5-8
©2000 by King Features Syndicate, Inc. World rights reserved.

TONIGHT'S FISTICUFF BATTLE WILL BE REFEREED BY THAT ACME OF HONESTY AND FAIRNESS, THE NOBLE J. WELLINGTON WIMPY!!
?
?
?
?
?
BOO!
THANK YOU!
BOO!
THANK YOU!
BOO!
BOO!
BOO!
5-9
BUD SAGENDORF
©2000 by King Features Syndicate, Inc. World rights reserved.
I WANT A FAIR FIGHT.... NOW SHAKE HANDS BEFORE THE CONTEST BEGINS!
OKAY!
©2000 by King Features Syndicate, Inc. World rights reserved.
?
POW!
5-10
BUD SAGENDORF
I SAID TO SHAKE HANDS AND YOU SMACKED POPEYE!
YEAH!
©2000 by King Features Syndicate, Inc. World rights reserved.
SIR! THE FIGHT DOES NOT START UNTIL THE BELL RINGS!
DID ANYONE SEE WHERE POPEYE LANDED
?
BOING!
BUD SAGENDORF
5-11
YOU SMACKED POPEYE OUT OF THE RING AND WE CAN'T FIND HIM!
YEAH!
©2000 by King Features Syndicate, Inc. World rights reserved.
IF HE ISN'T IN THE RING IN FIVE SECONDS YOU WIN!
ONE-
-TWO-THREE-FOUR--
I YAM HERE... LE'S FIGHT!
BUD SAGENDORF
5-12

LET'S GO, REFEREE!
ARE YOU QUITE SURE YOU ARE READY TO TAKE THE WORST BEATING IN YOUR LIFE?
YEAH! I YAM FIT LIKE A FIDDLE!
©2000 by King Features Syndicate, Inc. World rights reserved
THE REFEREE WOULD LIKE TO WAGER FIFTY THOUSAND ON BRUTUS!
PLEASE!
THUD!
BUD SAGENDORF
5-13

THAT WAS A SPLENDID BLOW! YOU DROVE HIM THROUGH THE RING FLOOR!
NOT QUITE!
5-15
?
THAT DOES IT!
THUMP!
BUD SAGENDORF
©2000 by King Features Syndicate, Inc. World rights reserved.

POPEYE IS OUT OF THE RING... START COUNTING!
HM?
5-16
©2000 by King Features Syndicate, Inc. World rights reserved.
I'LL HAVE TO CHECK THE RULES!
OUT OF THE RING... ON THE ROPES... FLAT ON CANVAS... HM?
?
?
THERE IS NOTHING ABOUT THROUGH AND UNDER THE RING!
RULES
BUD SAGENDORF

I FEAR, SIR... I SHALL HAVE TO COUNT YOU OUT!
?
©2000 by King Features Syndicate, Inc. World rights reserved.
START COUNTING! I HAVE MY LIFE SAVINGS ON BRUTUS!
?
?
ONE-TWO-THREE-
OH, JOY! I'M ABOUT TO BE WATERFRONT CHAMPION!
I'LL MAKE A FORTUNE!
5-17
BUD SAGENDORF

FIVE - SIX - SEVEN -
YOO-HOO, POPEYE -- I AM ABOUT TO BECOME CHAMPION!
HA! HA!
©2000 by King Features Syndicate, Inc. World rights reserved.
EIGHT- NINE--
?
POW
5-18
BUD SAGENDORF
YOU WERE SAVED BY THE BELL, MISTER BRUTUS!
BUD SAGENDORF
5-19
©2000 by King Features Syndicate, Inc. World rights reserved.
YOU BEAST! YOU STRUCK HIM!
?
?
DOESN'T YA WANT ME TA WIN?
OF COURSE NOT!! I BET MY LIFE SAVINGS ON BRUTUS TO WIN!
?
YOU BET ON BRUTUS?
YOU'RE SO LITTLE I PLAN TO MAKE A FORTUNE!
?
©2000 by King Features Syndicate, Inc. World rights reserved.
IF YOU HIT MY INVESTMENT AGAIN I'LL HATE YOU!
LADIES AN' GEN'LEMENS... I YAM ABOUT TO LOSE THIS FIGHT ON ACCOUNT OF LOVE IS MORE IMPORTINK THAN KNOCKIN' THE TAR OUT OF A BIG, DUMB SWAB LIKE BRUTUS!
$
5-20
BUD SAGENDORF
BEAUTIFUL!
?
SPLAT!
5-22
CAN'T I HIT HIM JUS' ONCE?
NO!
©2000 by King Features Syndicate, Inc. World rights reserved.
WHEN MY BOYFRIEND LOSES I'LL MAKE A MILLION DOLLARS!
?
BUD SAGENDORF

SMASH HIM, BRUTUS!
WHAT AM I DOING? I AM ROOTING AGAINST THE MAN I LOVE!
©2000 by King Features Syndicate, Inc. World rights reserved.
BECAUSE I BET MY LIFE SAVINGS ON BRUTUS IS NO EXCUSE!
MONEY ISN'T EVERYTHING!
KILL HIM, POPEYE!
SMASH BRUTUS!
?
5-23
BUD SAGENDORF

YA WANTS ME TA WIN?
OF COURSE! I LOVE YOU!
©2000 by King Features Syndicate, Inc. World rights reserved.
5-24
OKAY, BRUTUS, YOU ASKED FER IT! LE'S FIGHT!
?
PHOOEY!! WATASNOZZLE MADE ME SO SMALL I CAN'T REACH HIS KNOCK-OUT BUTTON!
HA! HA! HA! HA!! HA!
SWISH!
BUD SAGENDORF

BOXING TONIGHT
SMACK!
POW!
©2000 by King Features Syndicate, Inc. World rights reserved.
WATASNOZZLE! HELP!
?
?
YOU SHRUNK POPEYE SO MUCH HE CAN'T REACH BRUTUS' JAW!
AMAZING! I AM INDEED A TRUE GENIUS!
YA HAS'TA ENLARGE HIM!
5-25
BUD SAGENDORF

POPEYE'S ON THE ROPES! HELP HIM!
HM? I HAVE A BRILLIANT THEORY!
©2000 by King Features Syndicate, Inc. World rights reserved.
POPEYE HAS EATEN SO MUCH SPINACH THAT HE IS NO DIFFERENT THAN A VEGETABLE!
?
?
I'LL SPRAY HIM WITH MY SUPER-GROWTH PLANT FORMULA!
BUD SAGENDORF
5-26

WHA'CHA DOIN'?
I SPRAYED YOU WITH MY SUPER-GROWTH PLANT FORMULA!
©2000 by King Features Syndicate, Inc. World rights reserved.
THE SPINACH IN YOUR SYSTEM SHOULD MAKE YOU GROW TO YOUR NORMAL SIZE!
5-27
SHALL WE GIT ON WIT' THE FIGHT?
?
!
BUD SAGENDORF
HOW ABOUT IT, LITTLE FELLOW, SHALL WE FIGHT?
YOU MADE HIM A GIANT!
YOU WANTED HIM BIG!
!
PAT! PAT!
HELP!
MAMA!!
ARENA
5-29
BUD SAGENDORF
©2000 by King Features Syndicate, Inc. World rights reserved.
NOW YOU'VE MADE MY SAILOR BOY TOO BIG!
NOTHING TO WORRY ABOUT!
ARENA
5-30
©2000 by King Features Syndicate, Inc. World rights reserved.
MY FORMULA WORKS LIKE A BOUNCING BALL!
BUD SAGENDORF
SEE! HE'S BOUNCED BACK TO NORMAL SIZE!
?
AHOY, OLIVE, IS YA READY TA GO HOME?
YOU'RE BACK TO NORMAL!
YEAH! AN' I YAM STILL CHAMPION!
5-31
©2000 by King Features Syndicate, Inc. World rights reserved.
I YAM SORRY YA LORST YER LIFE SAVINGS BETTING ON BRUTUS!
BUD SAGENDORF
YOU CAD!!
YOU COST ME SEVENTEEN-FIFTY!
ARF! ARF! WE IS BOTH BACK TO NORMAL!
ARF!
ARF!

I YAM GLAD YA IS STILL WATERFRONT CHAMPION!
IT WAS A TOUGH FIGHT!
©2000 by King Features Syndicate, Inc. World rights reserved.
BUT YOU NEVER HIT BRUTUS ONCE!
6/1
'AT'S WHAT WAS TOUGH! HE HAD ALL OF THE FUN!
?
?
?

I'VE DECIDED MY IDEA OF REDUCING PEOPLE'S SIZE BY FIFTY PERCENT WAS A MISTAKE!
?
©2000 by King Features Syndicate, Inc. World rights reserved.
THEY WOULD ALL BE MY HEIGHT—
—AND I LIKE TO BE DISTINCT!
?
?
!
6-2

I WON ME SPRIZE-FIGHT WIT' BRUTUS!
WHAT TOOK YOU SO LONG!
©2000 by King Features Syndicate, Inc. World rights reserved.
I'VE BEEN WAITING FOR YOU!!
?
PHOOEY! WHAT A WAY TO CELEBRATE!
6-3

THE MERMAID

©2000 by King Features Syndicate, Inc. World rights reserved.
"FRESH FISH!" A FABLE PROVING A SKINNY GIRL CAN BE AS DESIRABLE AS A TUNA SALAD!
I YAM GOIN' FISHIN'... I'LL FURNISH DINNER TONIGHT!
!
?
PUFF!
PUFF!
PUFF!
PUFF!
!
POPEYE HAS GONE FISHING! I'LL NEED TWO MACKEREL AND SIX CANS OF SPINACH!
BUD SAGENDORF 6-5
©2000 by King Features Syndicate, Inc. World rights reserved.
THEY IS NOTHIN' LIKE FISHIN' TA REST A MAN'S SOUL!
YEAH!! IT IS REAL PEACEFUL!
ESPECIALLY IF YA IS CAREFUL TA NOT BAIT YER HOOK!!
6-6
BUD SAGENDORF
YA KIN GIT A GOOD REST FISHIN' IF YA DOESN'T BAIT YER HOOK!
Z Z Z
BUD SAGENDORF
YIKE!
?
A BITE?
©2000 by King Features Syndicate, Inc. World rights reserved.
6-7
I HAS HOOKED SUMPIN' AN' I DIDN'T BAIT ME HOOK!
?
?
?
WHA' TH'...?
HELP!
HELP!
BLUB!
6-8
BUD SAGENDORF
©2000 by King Features Syndicate, Inc. World rights reserved.

BLOW ME DOWN!? ME FISH IS TALKIN'!
?
?
?
HELP!
LET ME GO!! CUT YOUR LINE!
?
?
?
GET YOUR HOOK OUT OF MY HAIR!
6-9
©2000 by King Features Syndicate, Inc. World rights reserved.
I YAM SORRY I HOOKED YA!
YA SHOULDN'T BE SWIMMIN' SO FAR FROM SHORE!
HELP ME ABOARD, PLEASE!
6-10
YIKE! YOU IS A MERMAID!
?
WHAT DID YOU EXPECT... A TALKING HALIBUT?
FLOP!
©2000 by King Features Syndicate, Inc. World rights reserved.
YOU IS THE FIRST MERMAID I HAS EVER CAUGHT!!
YOU'RE THE FIRST LANDLUBBER I'VE EVER SEEN!
©2000 by King Features Syndicate, Inc. World rights reserved.
HM! YOU HAS A REAL FISH TAIL!!
?
?
I'VE NEVER SEEN LEGS BEFORE!
HOW STRANGE!
HOW DO YOU TELL WHICH ONE IS DOING WHAT?
6-12
IT HAS BEEN NICE TALKIN' TO YA, MISS MERMAID!
GOOD-BY!
?
GOOD-BY?
?
©2000 by King Features Syndicate, Inc. World rights reserved.
?
YOU CAN'T THROW ME BACK!! YOU CAUGHT ME..... I BELONG TO YOU!!
?
IT'S THE LAW OF THE LOWER SEA!
6-13

I CAN'T KEEP YOU... YOU IS A FREE GIRL --ER-- FISH-ER- ?
YOU CAUGHT ME!! I'M YOURS!!
OH, WOE!!
IF YOU THROW ME BACK I'LL BE DISGRACED!! I'LL BE SACRIFICED TO THE GREAT KING CRAB!
?
?
IT'S THE LAW OF THE OCEAN FLOOR!
6-14
BUD SAGENDORF
©2000 by King Features Syndicate, Inc. World rights reserved.
SLAM!
HM! POPEYE IS BACK FROM HIS DAY'S FISHING!
YOO-HOO! DID YOU CATCH ANY FISH?
©2000 by King Features Syndicate, Inc. World rights reserved.
BLOW ME DOWN!
'AT'S A BLASTID GOOD QUESTION!
?
6-15
BUD SAGENDORF
I ASKED YOU, DID YOU CATCH ANYTHING?
YEAH!! IT'S IN'A KITCHEN!
ERF!
!
?
?
I'LL HAVE TO HAVE A LARGER FRYING PAN IF YOU EXPECT ME TO COOK THIS!
?
!
?
?
6-16
BUD SAGENDORF
©2000 by King Features Syndicate, Inc. World rights reserved.
AHOY, SON... CATCH ANY FISH?
I CAUGHT ME A BIG ONE!
SHIVER ME TIMBERS! PORT ME HELM!
!
?
?
TUNA SALAD, WHAT IS YOU DOIN' HERE
?
POOPDECK PAPPY!!
WOW!
6-17
BUD SAGENDORF
©2000 by King Features Syndicate, Inc. World rights reserved.

WHO IS PAPPY TALKING TO ?
?
AN OL' FRIEN'!
BLA-BLA-- TEE-HEE-- BLA-BLA-
THAT DOESN'T SOUND VERY OLD TO ME !!
THAT'S NO OLD FRIEND!! THAT'S A BEAUTIFUL YOUNG GIRL!!
!
?
?
6-19
BUD SAGENDORF
©2000 by King Features Syndicate, Inc. World rights reserved.

WHAT ARE YOU DOING WITH A YOUNG LADY IN YOUR HOUSE ?
I CAUGHT HER !
HE HOOKED ME, SO I'M HIS!
©2000 by King Features Syndicate, Inc. World rights reserved.
I'LL KILL HER!!
!
6-20
BUD SAGENDORF

STOP, OLIVE! SHE AIN'T NO GIRL... SHE'S A FISH!
I'LL KILL HER!
A FISH ?
?
©2000 by King Features Syndicate, Inc. World rights reserved.
!
IF THAT'S A FISH, YOU'RE GOING TO TAKE UP GOLF!!
?
!
6-21
BUD SAGENDORF

SHE AIN'T A GIRL... SHE'S A MERMAID!
HA!
MERMAID! HA! HA!! THERE AIN'T NO SUCH ANIMAL!
!
©2000 by King Features Syndicate, Inc. World rights reserved.
?
?
?
THAT'S NOT TRUE !!
FLOP
6-22
BUD SAGENDORF

WHY DIDN'T YOU THROW IT BACK?
I TRIED, BUT SHE DOESN'T THROW!
HE CAUGHT ME, SO I BELONG TO HIM... IT'S THE LAW OF THE SEA!
GULP! DON'T MAKE HER MAD, OLIVE!!
-AND OLIVE'S LAW SAYS HE BELONGS TO ME!!
!
!
6-23
BUD SAGENDORF
©2000 by King Features Syndicate, Inc. World rights reserved.
DON'T MAKE HER MAD!
DON'T BE SILLY!! I'M NOT AFRAID OF AN OVERSIZED MACKEREL
MACKEREL!
NOW YA HAS DONE IT! SHE IS SINGIN'!
SHE SOUNDS LIKE A SICK BONITO!
WEE-eeeo!
OH-WEEeee!
6-24
BUD SAGENDORF
©2000 by King Features Syndicate, Inc. World rights reserved.
IT'S RAINING!
?
?
WEEEeeeow
YEEeeow!
©2000 by King Features Syndicate, Inc. World rights reserved.
BUD SAGENDORF
I TOLD YOU NOT TO MAKE HER MAD!
YA MADE HER SING UP A STORM!
6-26
YA MAKES A MERMAID MAD, AN' IT WILL SING UP A STORM!
SHE IS VERY SENSITIVE!
ALL I DID WAS CALL HER A MACKEREL!
MACKEREL!!
YEEeeow!
WEEEeeow!
6-27
BUD SAGENDORF
©2000 by King Features Syndicate, Inc. World rights reserved.

©2000 by King Features Syndicate, Inc. World rights reserved.
I TRUST POPEYE HAS LUNCH ON THE TABLE!
POPEYE
HM? POPEYE MUST HAVE A LEAKY TAP!
6-28
TUNA SALAD IS SINGIN' UP A BLASTID TYPHOON!
YOU WOULDN'T THINK CALLING HER A MACKEREL WOULD MAKE HER SO MAD!
MACKEREL!
OH!
WHEEEeeOW!
BUD SAGENDORF

I MUST TELL POPEYE THAT HE HAS DAMPNESS IN HIS HOUSE!
IT MUST BE A LEAKY TAP IN THE KITCHEN!
COME IN, WIMPY!
KNOCK!
!
?
6-29
BUD SAGENDORF
©2000 by King Features Syndicate, Inc. World rights reserved.

GOOD HEAVENS! POPEYE'S HOUSE WAS FULL OF WATER!
THANKS FER OPENING ME DOOR, WIMPY!
DO YOU KNOW YOU HAVE A LEAKY TAP, OL' PAL?
IT AIN'T NO LEAKY FAUCET... IT IS A MERMAID SINGIN' UP A STORM!
YEEEeeeow!
WAAAOW!
6-30
BUD SAGENDORF
©2000 by King Features Syndicate, Inc. World rights reserved.

OLIVE CALLED TH' MERMAID A MACKEREL, AN' SHE GOT MAD!
THE STORM IS OVER. SHE STOPPED SINGING!
?
?
?
HOW'D YA STOP HER?
I TOLD HER SHE LOOKED LIKE A GOLDFISH!
7-1
BUD SAGENDORF
©2000 by King Features Syndicate, Inc. World rights reserved.

MISS TUNA SALAD SANG UP A STORM IN POPEYE'S HOUSE ?
IT'S CHARACTERISTIC OF MERMAIDS!
MAKE THEM MAD AND YOU HAVE INSTANT RAIN!!
GOOD HEAVENS!! DO YOU REALIZE THE POTENTIAL OF SUCH A TALENTED FISH?
INDEED I DO!! SHE'S MUCH TOO PRETTY TO BE AROUND MY SAILOR!!
BUD SAGENDORF
7-3
©2000 by King Features Syndicate, Inc. World rights reserved.

©2000 by King Features Syndicate, Inc. World rights reserved.
WE CAN MAKE A FORTUNE, MISS OYL!
HOW ?
?
?
BY BORROWING POPEYE'S FISH!
MISS OYL AND I WOULD LIKE TO TAKE MISS TUNA SALAD FOR A WALK!
SHOW HER THE TOWN!
WALK? SHE AIN'T BUILT FOR WALKIN'!
!
?
7-4
BUD SAGENDORF

YA CAN'T TAKE TUNA SALAD WALKIN'! SHE AIN'T GOT NO FEETS!
MISS OYL AND I HAVE THAT LITTLE PROBLEM SOLVED!
?
?
?
?
BUT WHY TAKE A FISH FOR A WALK?
FOR FINANCIAL GAIN, MISS OYL!
7-5
BUD SAGENDORF
©2000 by King Features Syndicate, Inc. World rights reserved.

?
HOW DO WE MAKE MONEY WITH A MERMAID ?
PATIENCE, MISS OYL!
©2000 by King Features Syndicate, Inc. World rights reserved.
?
HOW ARE THE CROPS, MISTER THUMB ?
TERRIBLE!! AIN'T HAD NO RAIN IN TWO MONTHS!!
7-6
BUD SAGENDORF

YOU NEED RAIN ?
MY CABBAGES AND POTATOES ARE DYING!
I'D GIVE FIFTY DOLLARS FOR FIVE MINUTES OF RAIN!
?
INSULT MISS TUNA SALAD ENOUGH FOR A FIVE-MINUTE STORM!!
!
?
7-7
BUD SAGENDORF
©2000 by King Features Syndicate, Inc. World rights reserved.

GIVE HER A MILD INSULT AND WE'LL MAKE FIFTY BUCKS!
OKAY!
©2000 by King Features Syndicate, Inc. World rights reserved.
YOU REMIND ME OF A SMALL MACKEREL!
! !
WEEEeeoow! YEEeeow!!
SHE'S SINGING UP A MERMAID STORM!
THAT WILL BE FIFTY BUCKS!
RAIN!!
7-8
BUD SAGENDORF

QUITE A PROFITABLE DAY, MISS OYL!
TEN RAINSTORMS AT THREE HUNDRED APIECE!
PUFF!
LOOK HOW LOW THE CITY RESERVOIR IS!!
THEY'D PAY A LOT TO GET IT FILLED!
?
7-10
BUD SAGENDORF
©2000 by King Features Syndicate, Inc. World rights reserved.

OLIVE AN' WIMPY HAS HAD TUNA SALAD OUT FER A LONG WALK!!
©2000 by King Features Syndicate, Inc. World rights reserved.
PLOP!
THEY IS BACK!
BLOW ME DOWN, WIMPY! WHA'S WRONG WIT' HER ?
SHE'S TIRED, OL' PAL!
I FEAR WE GAVE HER TOO MUCH FRESH AIR!
ZZZ
BUD SAGENDORF
7-11

HOW KIN A MERMAID GIT EXHAUSTED FROM FRESH AIR?
THEY BREATHES IT ALL THE TIME!!
7-12
OLIVE AN' WIMPY MUST OF DONE MORE THAN JUS' TAKE HER FER A WALK!
WE GUARANTEE TO FILL THE CITY RESERVOIR WITH FRESH RAIN-WATER!
IT'LL ONLY TAKE A FEW HOURS AND A FEW THOUSAND DOLLARS!
?
?
H2O
WATERWORKS
BUD SAGENDORF
©2000 by King Features Syndicate, Inc. World rights reserved.
WE DO NEED WATER!
WE CAN FILL THE TOWN RESERVOIR!
DRIP
IT WOULD BE WORTH TEN THOUSAND DOLLARS TO HAVE A FULL RESERVOIR!
DO YOU THINK TUNA SALAD CAN SING UP A BIG ENOUGH STORM TO FILL A RESERVOIR?
SHE CAN IF YOU INSULT HER BIG ENOUGH!
BUT FIRST WE HAVE TO BORROW HER FROM POPEYE!
7-13
BUD SAGENDORF
©2000 by King Features Syndicate, Inc. World rights reserved
HOW IS TUNA SALAD?
SHE IS STILL EXHAUSTED FROM YA TAKIN' HER FER A WALK!!
MISS OYL AND I WOULD LIKE TO MAKE IT UP TO THE POOR FISH!
BUD SAGENDORF
©2000 by King Features Syndicate, Inc. World rights reserved.
WE'D LIKE TO TAKE HER FOR ANOTHER WALK!
HUH?
?
!
?
?
7-14
WIMPY AND I WOULD LIKE TO SHOW TUNA SALAD OUR TOWN RESERVOIR!!
BLOW ME DOWN!
SWELL!
'AT'S A GOOD IDEA! SHE MIGHT LIKE TO GO FER A SWIM!
?
SHE CAN SWIM AFTER SHE FILLS THE RESERVOIR!
SHE'LL HAVE TO SING UP A LARGE STORM TO DO THE JOB!
7-15
BUD SAGENDORF
©2000 by King Features Syndicate, Inc. World rights reserved.

I HOPES OLIVE AN' WIMPY SHOWS TUNA SALAD A GOOD TIME AT THE CITY RESERVOIR!
MERMAIDS IS MOSTLY FISH, SO THEY HAS TO HAVE A SWIM ONCE IN'A WHILE!
©2000 by King Features Syndicate, Inc. World rights reserved.
IT'LL TAKE HOURS TO FILL THE RESERVOIR!
?
?
SHE'LL NEED A BIG INSULT TO MAKE HER CRY UP A REAL MERMAID CLOUD-BURST!
7-17

I BET TUNA SALAD IS HAVIN' A NICE TIME AT THE RESERVOIR!
THEY AIN'T A BLASTID CLOUD IN'A SKY!
BLOW ME DOWN!?! I IS WRONG!!
?
THEY IS ONE BIG, NASTY CLOUD!! IT IS RIGHT OVER THE RESERVOIR!!
7-18
©2000 by King Features Syndicate, Inc. World rights reserved.

'AT STORM OVER THE RESERVOIR IS GO'NER SPOIL TUNA SALAD'S OUTING!
7-19
©2000 by King Features Syndicate, Inc. World rights reserved.
THE RESERVOIR IS QUITE FULL, WIMPY!
WOEeee!
YOU CAN STOP THE STORM NOW, MISS TUNA SALAD!
FLOP

'AT STORM OVER THE RESERVOIR IS STILL RAGIN'!
©2000 by King Features Syndicate, Inc. World rights reserved.
BLOW ME DOWN!? HERE COMES OLIVE AN' WIMPY!
?
FLOOD!
FLOOD!
FLOOD! TIDAL WAVE! FLOOD!
?
?
7-20

YOU WHAT ?
WE GOT TUNA SALAD TO CRY UP A STORM !
?
THE PROBLEM IS WE CAN'T STOP HER !
THEY ARE PAYING US TO FILL THE TOWN RESERVOIR !
?
I SUGGEST WE GET TO HIGHER GROUND.... THE FLOOD IS STARTING TO ARRIVE!
BUD SAGENDORF
7-21
©2000 by King Features Syndicate, Inc. World rights reserved.

THE ONLY WAY YA KIN GIT A MERMAID TA CRY UP A STORM IS TO INSULT HER !
I KNOW !
©2000 by King Features Syndicate, Inc. World rights reserved.
WE'RE GOING TO GET PAID FOR FILLING THE RESERVOIR !
WHAT DID YA SAY TA THE POOR GIRL-FISH TA GIT A FLOOD LIKE THIS ?
TEE-HEE ! I TOLD HER SHE HAD A FIGURE LIKE A HALIBUT !!
BUD SAGENDORF
7-22

EVERY-THIN' IS UN'ER WATER !
SO WHAT? WE HAD A JOB TO DO !
WIMPY AND I ARE GETTING TEN THOUSAND DOLLARS FOR FILLING THE RESERVOIR !
CITY HALL
-AND AFTER WE PAY.... WE'RE SUING YOU FOR ONE MILLION DOLLARS FOR FLOODING THE TOWN !!
MAYOR
?
?
!
BUD SAGENDORF
7-24
©2000 by King Features Syndicate, Inc. World rights reserved.

YA BETTER STOP TUNA SALAD SINGIN' OR SHE WILL FLOOD THE WHOLE COUNTRY !
I TRIED!
SHE'S A VERY SENSATIFF MERMAID AN' YA OVERDID YER INSULK!
?
SOMEBODY HAS TO STOP HER SINGIN' UP A STORM B'FORE WE HAS'TA BUILD AN ARK !
BUD SAGENDORF
7-25
©2000 by King Features Syndicate, Inc. World rights reserved.

©2000 by King Features Syndicate, Inc. World rights reserved.
AVAST! STOP YER BLASTID SINGIN'! YA IS FLOODIN' THE TOWN!!
SHE SAID I HAD A FIGURE LIKE A HALIBUT!!
WOOEEEee!
SHE WAS JUS' BEIN' MEAN! I THINKS YA IS TH' MOS' BEAUTIFUL FISH I HAS EVER SEED!
YOU DO? WOW!! HOW WONDERFUL! YOU THINK I'M BEAUTIFUL!
WOW!
GOSH!!
7-26
BUD SAGENDORF
HOT DORG! YA HAS STOPPED SINGIN' UP A STORM... THE SUN IS OUT!
YOU SAID I'M BEAUTIFUL!
I CAN'T SING UP A STORM WHEN MY HEART IS FULL OF LOVE AND JOY!
I HAVE TO FIND DADDY AND TELL HIM HIS FAVORITE DAUGHTER IS GETTING MARRIED!!
BLOW ME DOWN!?
?
?
7-27
BUD SAGENDORF
©2000 by King Features Syndicate, Inc. World rights reserved.
THE WATER IS GOING DOWN!
POPEYE MUST HAVE STOPPED TUNA SALAD!
HERE HE COMES... HOW DID YOU STOP HER?
?
?
?
?
I TOLD HER SHE WAS A BEAUTIFUL FISH--
AN' NOW I THINKS I YAM ENGAGED TO A BLASTID MERMAID!
?
7-28
BUD SAGENDORF
©2000 by King Features Syndicate, Inc. World rights reserved.
YOU CAN'T BE ENGAGED!! YOU'RE PROMISED TO ME!!
BLOW ME DOWN!! 'AT'S WHAT I TRIED TO TELL HER!
BUT SHE SAID SHE WAS GOIN' HOME TO TELL HER DADDY WE WAS GITTIN' MARRIED!
OL' PAL...IF YOU MARRY A MERMAID YOU'LL HAVE TO HONEYMOON UNDER WATER!!
SHE SAID IF I DIDN'T MARRY HER SHE'D CRY UP A STORM AN' DROWN THE WHOLE WORLD!
?
?
7-29
BUD SAGENDORF
©2000 by King Features Syndicate, Inc. World rights reserved.

GOOD HEAVENS!? WHAT IS POPEYE DOING?
?
HE'S WORRIED!
SO HE'S PRACTICING!
IF HE'S GOING TO SAVE THE WORLD BY MARRYING A MERMAID, HE HAS TO LEARN TO LIVE UNDER-WATER!!
!
-SIX MINUTES FORTY SECONDS-
BLUB!
7-31
BUD SAGENDORF
©2000 by King Features Syndicate, Inc. World rights reserved.
AREN'T YOU UPSET ABOUT POPEYE MARRYING A MERMAID?
NOT AT ALL!
POPEYE CAUGHT TUNA SALAD WITH A LINE AND HOOK!
!
?
SO I'M GOING FISHING!!
AND WHEN I CATCH HER I'LL TURN HER INTO CAT FOOD!
BAIT
8-1
BUD SAGENDORF
©2000 by King Features Syndicate, Inc. World rights reserved.
YOU'RE NOT REALLY GOING TO MARRY A MERMAID?
I HAS TA SAVE THE WORLD FROM BEIN' FLOODED!
IF I MAKES HER MAD SHE'LL CRY UP A STORM AN' DROWN US ALL!
©2000 by King Features Syndicate, Inc. World rights reserved.
BUT, OL' PAL... YOU'RE PROMISED TO MISS OYL!
YIKE!?! TUNA SALAD IS BACK!!
SHE IS CALLIN' ME!
POPEYE!
POPEYE!
8-2
BUD SAGENDORF
WHAT'S POPEYE DOING?
?
?
TUNA SALAD CALLED HIM AND THEY'RE HAVING A CHAT!
I THINK SHE'S SETTING THE DATE FOR THEIR WEDDING!
NEGOTIATIONS SEEM TO BE PROGRESSING!
OH! WOE!
YAS! YAS! OKAY! YAS! YAS! I WILL! YAS! YAS!
-AND-
8-3
BUD SAGENDORF
©2000 by King Features Syndicate, Inc. World rights reserved.

IT IS ALL SET.... I YAM GO'NER MARRY TUNA SALAD!
YOU CAN'T! YOU BELONG TO ME!
YA AIN'T GOT NOTHIN' TA WORRY ABOUT, OLIVE!
ARF!
MERMAIDS LIVES A LONG TIME --
-SHE WANTS TA WAIT FER HER SIX-HUN'REDTH BIRTHDAY ... I AGREED ON ACCOUNT OF 'AT AIN'T UNTIL THE YEAR OF 2096!
BY THEN I YAM SURE SHE WILL CHANGE HER MIND!
8-4
©2000 by King Features Syndicate, Inc. World rights reserved.

YOU GOT RID OF TUNA SALAD, BUT WHAT ABOUT WIMPY AN' ME?
?
THE CITY IS SUING US FOR ONE MILLION DOLLARS FOR THE FLOOD!
-SO-BILL 'EM A MILLING BUCKS FER WASHIN' THE STREETS!
ARF!
8-5
©2000 by King Features Syndicate, Inc. World rights reserved.

SPINACH